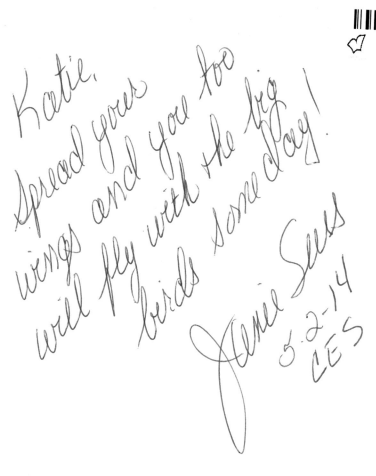

Katie,
Spread your
wings and you too
will fly with the big
birds some day!

Jennie Sews
5-2-14
CES

OSCAR AND OLIVE
OSPREY

A Family Takes Flight

JANIE SUSS

Synergy Books

Oscar and Olive Osprey: A Family Takes Flight
Published by Synergy Books
PO Box 80107
Austin, TX 78758

For more information about our books, please write to us, call 512.478.2028, or visit our website at www.synergybooks.net.

Publisher's Cataloging-in-Publication
(Provided by Quality Books, Inc.)

Suss, Janie.
    Oscar and Olive Osprey : a family takes flight /
Janie Suss.
    p. cm.
    SUMMARY: Describes the daily life and habitat of two
ospreys that come to live at the end of the author's
pier on a platform built just for them. Janie watches as
the two birds build their nest, raise three babies,
defend themselves against predators, and as each baby
bird grows and learns at its own pace within the family.
    Audience: Ages 9-12.
    LCCN 2009927846
    ISBN-10: 978-0-9823140-6-7
    ISBN-13: 0-9823140-6-X

    1. Osprey--Maryland--Juvenile literature.
2. Families--Juvenile literature. 3. Chesapeake Bay (Md.
and Va.)--Juvenile literature. [1. Osprey. 2. Family
life. 3. Chesapeake Bay (Md. and Va.)]   I. Title.

QL696.F36S87 2010   598.9'3752
                    QBI09-600106

Visit www.oscarandolive.com for updates and events.

10 9 8 7 6 5 4 3 2

To my children, Gus and Sadie, who have given
me precious memories of watching them learn,
and seeing them grow. They have given me
all the love and rewards of motherhood. They
have left the nest and made wonderful lives
of their own, and I am so proud of them.

Contents

Acknowledgements

Getting to know Oscar and Olive has been inspiring in itself. I have watched and learned so much. Without my neighbors' help in putting up the platform, I would not have been able to experience the joy I have had in getting to know Oscar and Olive and watching them raise their family. I want to say thank you to Danny for getting us started and to Doug and Bradley for the finished product.

I would also like to thank my husband, who didn't believe the platform would work, but who built it for me without complaining. He appreciates my childlike ways and my enthusiasm for the simple things in life. He has been very supportive and helpful every step of the way, and I love him dearly for that.

I would especially like to say thank you to Janet McGuire, more fondly known as Aunt Janet. I could tell she felt the same excitement I felt when she would ask about "my birds." Without her encouragement and confidence in me as a storyteller, what I have learned and captured in my heart by knowing Oscar and Olive would have been left untold.

Last but not least, I would like to thank my family: my older brother and younger brother, my older sisters, and my younger sisters, for teaching me when there were lessons to be taught, learning from me when there was something to learn, and being there for me and for each other. And thank you to Mom and Dad for their love and for setting the perfect example. They have instilled in each one of us the true meaning of the word "family."

Introduction

Hi! My name is Janie, or as my neighbors call me, "Bird Woman." I make sure that in my yard the wild birds have food,

shelter, and even a place to wash, get a drink of water, or just cool themselves. My oversized birdbath is for all the birds, even the big, black crows! I have bird feeders that attract cardinals, chickadees, nuthatches, purple finches, and just about any other hungry bird that comes along. The goldfinches like to eat hanging upside down, so they have their own feeder with their own special seed. You'll see the blue jays come down to the porch to get a peanut, take it high up in the tree, crack it open, and enjoy the treat they find inside. The mourning doves show up in pairs to get their share. They like the seed that has fallen to the ground. I even have two hummingbird feeders with sugar-water that gives the little guys the energy they need to flap their wings so fast. I also have a birdhouse with sixteen separate "apartments" for the purple martins. They make it their happy home every year. They fly and dive like acrobats over the land and water, catching insects in the early mornings and every evening. I love all the birds around here, but my newest and most exciting ones are the ospreys. They have been seen in almost all parts of the world and are sometimes called sea hawks or fish hawks. On the Chesapeake Bay, in the state of Maryland, they are called ospreys, and there is a pair of ospreys that live at the end of my pier on a platform built just for them.

I have lived on the waters of the Chesapeake Bay all my life. These beautiful birds that make nests out of piles of sticks have always fascinated me. They build nests on top of telephone poles,

towers, and tops of old trees, but I have mostly seen them on channel markers out in the water. Ospreys that live on the Chesapeake Bay are running out of places near the water to build nests, so people have started helping by putting up posts with nest platforms on top. I'm really excited to write about these birds, because I have come to know two of them very well. I have even named them: Oscar and Olive Osprey. I'd like you to get to know them, too.

Chapter 1

ABOUT OSPREYS

Ospreys are big, beautiful birds. Adult ospreys can be as long as two feet from the top of their heads to the end of their tails, and when they spread their wings, they can be as wide as six feet from the tip of one wing to the tip of the other! Their backs and wings are brown, their breasts are white streaked with brown, and their undersides are white. Their heads are white with a dark streak across their eyes all the way to the sides of their neck.

They look like they have a mask on over their golden eyes. This dark mask helps to keep the sun's glare from shining too brightly in their eyes, like sunglasses or the black marks football players put under their eyes when playing in the sun. Ospreys' beaks are black, and their feet are white with black talons (which is the fancy name for a bird's claws). Their tails are short, and they have long, narrow wings that bend in the middle like a seagull's wings. On the end, there are four long feathers and a shorter fifth. This wing shape is one way you can tell the osprey from other large birds when he flies. Male and female ospreys are almost the same, except females are a little bit bigger and more streaked on the breast. This difference is so small that it is hard to tell a male from a female unless they are sitting next to each other. The way they glide high in the sky, hunting for fish, reminds me of a kite flying.

Ospreys live on the water because they mainly eat fish. If they can't find fish, which is usually rare, they will eat salamanders or small reptiles. They will fly as high as 130 feet in the air to look for a fish, then dive straight down into the water, feet first, and catch it. Their eyes are very powerful, so they can see through the water from that high up. If the fish is close to the surface, the osprey will make a quick catch on the top of the water. If the fish is underwater and moves slowly, the osprey will dive as deep as three feet to get him. An osprey has a special nose that will close up when he dives into the water so that water doesn't get in.

After he catches his fish, the osprey flies back up in the sky and does a couple of shakes to get rid of the water, much like a dog. Then he starts whistling and chirping over and over again as if he is telling everyone, "I caught a fish!" If he has a mate, he will fly high over her head just to show her his fish. If you look at the fish he is carrying, you will see that it is always gripped by the talons and facing forward. This is because the osprey can fly faster when the fish is facing the same direction he is. His feet are different from any other bird to make it easy for him to catch and carry the fish this way.

Now that you know a little about this beautiful bird, I'd like to tell you how Oscar and Olive Osprey made their home at the end of my pier.

Chapter 2

FINDING A PLACE TO CALL HOME

When I have been out on boats on the Chesapeake Bay, I have noticed that when you get close to an osprey nest on a channel marker, they aren't bothered. They will look right back at you, just like you are looking at them. Where I live, there is a pier with poles along the side and the front so you can tie up a boat if you want to dock it there. There is no boat at my pier, but there is one pole that is a little taller and is out a little farther than the others. When I noticed the taller pole, I thought maybe an osprey family would like to live there. When I told my friends that I wanted to put a platform out there for ospreys to build a nest on, they told me I was crazy. But I didn't care what anyone else thought. I just had to try it. So I got the things I needed to build a platform. Using boards made of recycled material that wouldn't be hurt by the weather, my husband and I built a frame to support a platform. Then, using screws that wouldn't rust, we attached boards across the frame with one-inch spaces between each board for drainage and air flow. When we were finished, the platform was about four feet long and four feet wide. Finally, we put wire

around the edge to help hold the first few sticks in place. If the ospreys liked it, it would be great! If they didn't, well, then at least I had tried.

My neighbors helped me put the platform up even though they didn't think it would work. I knew I had waited too late in the season for a pair of ospreys to build a nest and lay eggs that season, but I hoped that someone would claim it as a starter home for next spring. We put it up in the evening, and guess what? The very next morning when I woke up, there was an osprey on the platform! I was so excited. I called my neighbors right away. I didn't care how early it was—everyone had to know! I could hardly get ready for work because I was watching his every move. If he flew away, I'd watch and wait for him to come back. When he came back, I'd watch to see how long he stayed. Then he came back with a stick! Had he decided the platform would be a good place for a nest?

He brought another stick and another and another. He had brought four sticks! This was great! Then he brought another four sticks, one by one, and now there were eight sticks on the platform. This osprey was ready to make this platform his home! I had to go to work, but when I came home later that day, there were so many sticks I couldn't count them. It had worked! He was building a nest on my platform. I decided right then that he needed a name. I was going to call him Oscar. Oscar Osprey.

Chapter 3

FINDING A MATE

Oscar spent a lot of time on the platform, bringing in sticks and arranging them to make his nest. Ospreys use sticks, big and small, grasses, small branches with leaves on them, string, and just about anything they can find to make a nest. I have even seen

osprey nests with old fishing line and plastic bags.

There were other ospreys flying around at the same time, looking for a place to nest. They wanted to take over and have the new platform as their home. They would try to land, and Oscar would chase them away. Sometimes there were as many as three other ospreys diving at Oscar and chasing him, trying to take over the platform, but Oscar showed them who was boss. He had found his new home, and no one was going to take it away.

After a few days, the other ospreys didn't come around as often, but there was one that Oscar would let land on the platform. When the two of them were standing there together, I noticed that the other osprey was a little bigger and wondered if Oscar was going to give in to the bigger bird. I hoped Oscar had not given up. Then it all came together. Oscar had not only found a home but had found a mate! All of this happened in just a few days. It had worked! I had a male and female osprey to live on my platform. It was not only a happy time for me but a happy time for Oscar. I named his mate Olive, and that's how I met Oscar and Olive Osprey.

I put the platform up on July 11, which was well into the summer months. Even though Oscar and Olive had made this their home, it would be too late for them to have babies. The baby ospreys need enough time to grow up and get strong before the cold weather comes, so they can fly south where it's warm. But for now, Oscar and Olive were letting the other ospreys know that this was their home. They had started a nest to come back to next year.

Chapter 4

VACATIONING IN THE WARM SOUTH

Ospreys have been seen all over the world except in Antarctica. If they live in a place where it is warm all year round, they just stay where they are, but in Maryland, they go south in late August and early September. If they have babies, the parents teach their young to fly and catch fish, and then leave them behind when they go south. When the babies get stronger and can catch fish, then they will also go south, usually only a couple of weeks after their parents leave. When the parents go south, they will go as far as South America and then come back to Maryland around the middle of March. (It has been said that you can always start looking for the osprey to return starting March 17, St. Patrick's Day.) The pair of ospreys will not stay together while they are away in the south, but they will always meet back at the same nest at about the same time the next year. Then they have their babies for that season.

The babies that go south for the first time only go as far as Florida, and they stay there until they are one or two years old. Then they fly back to the place they were born. If they are lucky, they will find a place to nest and a mate the first year they come home. If they don't, they will come back the next year and try again. It usually takes them a couple of years to nest and find a mate, so most osprey pairs don't start having babies until they are three or four years old. In Maryland, on the Chesapeake Bay, most ospreys don't start having babies until they are five, six, or even seven years old, because it is so hard to find a place to nest. Putting up platforms like mine is a great way to help the ospreys find a good home. When a pair of ospreys makes a nest together, they will stay together as a pair, and it will be their nest every year for the rest of their lives. Ospreys can live to be twenty to twenty-five years old!

This is what Oscar and Olive did. They found each other and a place to call home. For the rest of the warm summer months, they stayed together and worked on the nest. Oscar would bring most of the sticks to the platform, and Olive would arrange them perfectly so they would not fall off. It was coming along really well, and even though other ospreys would come by occasionally and try to take over, Oscar and Olive would protect their nest.

Olive would stay on the nest, and Oscar would chase the others away. Oscar and Olive took good care of each other and protected their new home.

September came, and with the cooler weather coming in, Oscar and Olive knew it was time to go south. They weren't just out fishing or gone from their nest for a little while—they were gone for the winter. I missed hearing their whistling and squawking and watching them build their nest.

Chapter 5

IT'S WINTER AND NOBODY'S HOME

As the winter went on, with all its storms, wind, snow, and ice, Oscar and Olive's nest stayed in place and didn't lose a stick. Oscar and Olive had put each one in just the right place. They had built their nest to last, and I didn't realize how true

that was until I saw it for myself. It was like the sticks were glued together. I don't know what their secret is, but it works.

During the winter, there was someone else who enjoyed the platform. It was an American bald eagle. I knew they lived in this area, and I would see them flying by once in a while, but when they found Oscar and Olive's platform, the eagles liked it, too. Most of the time, eagles use tall trees for nesting and like to live *near* the water, not on platforms *over* the water. Eagles like to eat fish and small ducks, but living on the land makes it easier for them to also find muskrats, turtles, rabbits, snakes, and other small animals to eat.

Oscar and Olive's nest was not as big as other osprey nests yet, but to another bird as big as an eagle, it was a great place to land over the water to eat or rest. It was high, and they had a clear view of things around them so they could keep watch and feel safe. If this were the summer months and Oscar and Olive were here, the eagles would never land on the platform. Oscar and Olive wouldn't let them, not only because it is their home, but because eagles and ospreys do not get along. If an eagle comes

close to an osprey or his nest, the osprey will do everything he can to chase the eagle away. When Oscar and Olive come back to the Chesapeake Bay, the eagles will stay away from them. Knowing what the eagles like to eat, it makes sense that the ospreys don't like having the eagles around. An unprotected baby osprey might be just what the eagle would like to have for dinner that day!

As it gets colder and the winter comes in, thousands of winter ducks come to the Chesapeake Bay. They float together in large groups called "rafts" because from far away they look like large black spots in the water, just like a big raft. Others will just swim around by themselves. Most of the ducks are small enough for an eagle to fly by and pick one up for dinner. So while Oscar and Olive were vacationing in the warm south for the long, cold winter months, the winter ducks and eagles put on quite a show. The same pair of eagles enjoyed the osprey platform that whole winter. They are such beautiful birds and wonderful to watch, so I had to give them names too! I named them Edward and Edith Eagle.

Chapter 6

HOME
SWEET HOME

For five months out of the year, starting in the spring, osprey pairs come home and start repair work on their nests. It was March 17, St. Patrick's Day, when the ospreys are known to return to the Chesapeake Bay, but I had not seen any sign of Oscar and Olive yet. I had seen other ospreys here and there, but not at the nest Oscar and Olive started last year. Another

week went by and still no Oscar and Olive. I watched and watched every day. I had waited all winter for them to come back, and I hoped I would see them soon. Then one day when I was coming down the driveway, I looked out to the platform, and there was Oscar, standing right in the middle of the small nest. But where was Olive? Maybe she was a little late getting here, just like Oscar. I hoped she would show up soon, and sure enough, she did. But she was not alone.

There were other ospreys that were trying to find a nesting place. Sometimes there would be four or five of them flying overhead, trying to land on the platform. Oscar and Olive would dive straight at them to chase them away. Olive would stay at the nest most of the time to guard it, while Oscar went to fish or get sticks and things for their nest. If Olive saw or sensed trouble,

she would whistle over and over very loud, and Oscar would come right away, diving and chasing the other ospreys away. It took a while for the other ospreys to finally leave them alone. Oscar and Olive were a great pair. Both did their parts protecting and building their home. They had to get ready for their first full season together on my platform.

I was also doing my spring repair work. I was putting down grass seed in my yard. After I put down the seed, I covered it with straw so the birds wouldn't eat the new seed. The straw had been tied together with an orange nylon string. I had almost thrown it away, but then I thought, "Maybe Oscar and Olive would like this for their nest." I've seen string in other osprey nests, so I left it right there on the ground. The next day, Oscar came swooping down to pick something up. But it wasn't the string. He picked up the straw. I hadn't even thought of that. Straw would help Oscar and Olive keep their eggs warm until they hatched. I said it before, and I'll say it again: Oscar and Olive sure know how to build a nest! Not long after that, the string disappeared from the yard. I looked out at the nest and there it was. Oscar and Olive thought it was a good idea, too.

There is a very large oak tree in my yard near Oscar and Olive's nest. It drops sticks all the time, especially after a storm, and I always pick them up. I used to put them in the woods, but now that Oscar and Olive were here, I took the sticks and put them on the rocks along the water or put them in one area on the grass so they could come and get them. It is really something to see them fly down to the ground without landing and do a quick stick pick-up. Watching the ospreys living on the Chesapeake Bay

is one thing, but to have Oscar and Olive as my neighbors is very special. With the sticks I put out, the straw I put down, and the string I left on the ground, I watched Oscar and Olive build their home sweet home.

Chapter 7

THERE ARE EGGS!

Olive was getting ready to lay her eggs for the first time. Oscar and Olive put the finishing touches on the inside of the nest. Oscar would bring grass, moss, or straw to Olive so she could put them in the bottom of the nest. These things would help hold heat. It was still a little bit cold this time of the year, so Olive had to make sure the nest would be a nice warm place for her eggs.

Oscar was flying overhead on his way home to the nest at the end of the day, and as I watched him, I saw something I hadn't seen before. He was missing a feather. It was one of the long feathers on his left wing, so I could easily see that it was missing. What had happened that day that made Oscar lose his wing feather? Had he run into some trouble or had it just fallen out? Oscar had no problem flying without that feather, and he was still able to do all the things he needed to do to take care of himself and Olive. Only now, when there were several ospreys flying around, I could tell which one was Oscar. Of course, Olive always knew. He was the one chirping and whistling in her direction. But for me, he was the one missing a feather!

After the first month went by, the nest was just right for having babies. And sure enough, Oscar came home one day and saw that Olive had laid an egg! Oscar and Olive were finally going to have the family they had worked so hard to get ready for. Then, two days later, Olive laid *another* egg, and by the end of the week—surprise!—she had even laid one more. Oscar and Olive had not only started their family, they were going to have a big family. They were so proud and so happy, looking down at their eggs, counting one, two, three. Each egg was a little smaller than a chicken egg. They were not really white, but almost white, and had reddish-brown splotches on them. Olive was now very happy to stay at home and spend her time sitting on the nest to keep her eggs safe and warm.

Chapter 8

HELPING, CLEANING, CARING

Oscar had his job, too. He would still bring sticks to the nest, but he brought fish most of the time. He made sure that Olive had plenty to eat and that she was happy sitting on the eggs. When Olive was hungry and Oscar was not around, she would whistle and chirp until he brought her fish. Then Olive would take the fish up in the trees to eat. Oscar and Olive liked my big oak tree. It was close to their nest and they could sit up high in the tree while eating and watching the nest at the same time. While Olive was away eating, Oscar would sit on the eggs to be sure they stayed warm. Oscar was a big help to Olive and always did his part.

When Olive was finished eating, she would fly around, get some exercise, stretch her wings, and wash her feet. Yes, wash her feet. She just ate a fish with them, and she wanted them to be clean before she went back to sit on the nest. Olive would fly only inches above the water so her feet would glide through the water and get clean. Oscar would do the same thing after he ate. It was important to keep themselves and their nest clean.

One afternoon, it started getting really dark and cloudy. A big storm was heading our way with strong winds and a lot of rain. Storms can get really bad when they come across a big body of water like the Chesapeake Bay. Olive had just come back from eating, and it was time for her to take over sitting on the eggs. It was getting pretty nasty out. Oscar flew off and settled in a protected area in a tree. He could still see Olive and would watch over her while she stayed at the nest to protect her eggs

during the storm. He would also be ready to fish for her when it was over.

The day turned into night, and the storm was getting worse. The strong winds had gusts of forty-five to fifty miles per hour. It was making the rain go sideways, and the bay water was very rough. The water was splashing up high on the rocks. Olive was sitting so low in the nest that you couldn't even tell she was there. Soon it got dark, and I couldn't see the nest or the platform at

all, but I could still hear that awful howling wind and the rain beating on the windows. The storm kept waking me through the night. I wondered how Olive was doing keeping her eggs warm and dry.

When the morning came, the storm had calmed, and I was glad to see that Olive and the nest were still there. Olive was still sitting very low. The rain finally stopped, and the clouds started to clear. Olive sat a little taller in the nest to have a look around. She decided it was safe now, and it was time to eat. She didn't have to make much noise before Oscar was right there. He knew Olive would be tired and hungry. After seeing that Olive and the eggs were okay, he hurried off to get some fish. When he came back with breakfast, Olive flew off into the trees to eat and Oscar took over sitting on the nest. Olive was a good mom and Oscar knew that. He took very good care of her.

Chapter 9

FROM OSCAR AND OLIVE TO MOM AND DAD

The summer days are very hot, and the nights get cool. Oscar and Olive both helped to keep their eggs at the right temperature. The eggs could not get too hot or too cold. Oscar knew that just sitting on the eggs wasn't enough. When Olive was sitting on them, they would be warm on the top, but what about the bottom? So when he would come to the nest and Olive would leave, Oscar would use his beak and gently turn each egg over and then settle in and sit on them just like Olive did to keep them warm.

Five weeks had gone by, and Oscar and Olive started checking their eggs closely every day for signs that their babies would be hatching soon. One day, Oscar was turning the first egg when he saw a tiny hole in the shell. He looked a little closer and there was also a small crack! It wouldn't be long now. He checked the second egg as he turned it over and then the third egg. He didn't see any other holes or cracks. There was no telling what would happen before Olive returned. Oscar knew it was still important to keep all three of them warm, so he gently sat on them like he always did. All he could think was, "Hurry home, Olive!" Olive soon came back, and Oscar was happy to let Olive take over.

All Olive could do was watch over the eggs and wait. Her babies had to hatch themselves with no help, and she knew they would come out of their shells when they were ready. It was a warm summer day when the first egg hatched. When the babies hatch, they weigh only two ounces and are one to two inches long. That is about the size of your mom's thumb. That is very tiny for a bird that will grow so big. As the days went by, the other eggs hatched in the same order Olive had laid them. Two days after the first one, the second one hatched, and by the end of the week all three tiny, fuzzy babies had hatched and were chirping away, begging for food. They were no longer just Oscar and Olive—they were Mom and Dad!

Chapter 10

WAS THAT A WITCH?

When Oscar would bring a fish to Olive, she wouldn't leave the nest anymore; she would share the fish. She would tear off tiny bites of fish and feed her babies deep inside the nest. Oscar and Olive shared the responsibilities of taking care of them. Oscar would do the fishing, and Olive would do the feeding. They would take turns sitting with their new babies for warmth and protection. When the babies are this small, they need more protection than warmth. It was now the end of May and into June, and the hotter days of summer were here. I started seeing more birds, fish, insects, and other animals that love the warmer months. One bird that enjoys all these things is the great blue heron.

The great blue heron is a very big bird. It can be three to five feet tall, and when it spreads its wings, they can measure up to six feet from one tip to the other. The great blue heron is blue-gray all over with a dull yellow bill and gray legs. They nest in trees or bushes near the water. They eat mostly small fish, but they are also known to eat shellfish, insects, frogs, snakes, small animals, and *small birds*. That's the scary part. Oscar and Olive knew this and had to always be on the watch.

It was a beautiful, quiet morning, and Olive was watching over her new babies. She saw that a large bird was flying toward them and coming very fast. She called for Oscar. It was an emergency. Oscar heard her and came quickly. Then there was a noise: an awful, low, hoarse croak. Olive knew exactly what it was. It was the great blue heron. You can usually find the heron fishing along the water's edge, but this heron was flying over the deeper water near Oscar and Olive's nest. Olive wasn't sure what the heron was going to do. Oscar came diving straight at the heron to chase her down into the water and away from the nest. Oscar would squawk at her with every dive, and the heron

would scream and croak right back. Back and forth, back and forth, they would scream and croak and squawk in the chase. The great blue heron is a bigger bird, but Oscar could dive very fast and could outsmart her in a lot of ways. Olive stayed with her babies and made just as much noise as Oscar did while he was

chasing the heron. Oscar and Olive did not like the heron. They knew if the great blue heron had a chance, she would make one of their babies her lunch!

When the great blue heron flies, it flaps its large, gray wings with big, slow strokes. It has a long, pointed bill, a long neck, and long, skinny legs. When it flies, it stretches its long neck out in front and its long, skinny legs out in back. When I see it and hear it make that awful, screaming, croaking noise, it reminds me of a witch screaming loudly as she is flying by on a broomstick, and that can only mean trouble. Unlike Edward and Edith Eagle, who stayed away and left Oscar and Olive alone while they were home

with their new babies, the heron stayed around. Sometimes in the night I would hear Oscar and the heron doing battle. Sneaking up on Oscar and Olive's nest was impossible even at night, and the heron learned this lesson very fast. I decided this great blue heron needed a name, too, and Harriett Heron seemed like a good name for this bird that reminded me so much of a witch.

Chapter 11

BABY NAMES

It wasn't long before Oscar and Olive's new tiny babies were big enough to peek out of the nest. They would stretch out their necks as far as they could, chirp as loud as they could, and open their mouths begging for food. Oscar had his work cut out for him feeding Olive and their three little babies. The babies were growing so fast. It was no wonder they ate all the time. Oscar would bring fish all day. The minute the sun came up, Olive and her babies would start peeping and begging. If there was a day with a lot of wind

and the water was rough, or if it was a rainy, stormy day, it was harder for Oscar to fish and feed everyone, but they always got fed. Oscar knew just how much fish he needed to catch to feed his family and keep them healthy and happy. Olive could always depend on him.

Olive would protect the babies from storms and the hot summertime sun. If it got too cold for them, she would keep them warm with her warm body. If it was a hot, sunny day, she would stand over them with her wings spread halfway to give them shade, like a big sun umbrella! Olive would stand there for hours, and as the sun moved, she would move to keep them in the shade. Oscar and Olive's babies were very sensitive to the

sun because they were so little and had only a soft, white fuzz on them to protect their little bodies. Even after two weeks when their feathers started coming in, it wasn't enough protection from the sun's hot rays.

There was one more thing. Oscar and Olive needed to give each one of their new babies a name. They started with the first one. He was a boy. What would be a good name for him? How about Omar, Omar Osprey? That was a good name. Omar was a

good name for a big brother. Even though he was only a few days older than the other two, he was still a big brother.

The second one was a girl. This one was easy. Olivia, Olivia Osprey. Olivia is such a beautiful name, and Olivia would one day grow up to be a beautiful bird! How lucky Olivia was to have Omar as a big brother to look up to and learn from.

Then there was the third baby. He was also a boy. He hatched last, and even though Omar hatched only about five days earlier, he had gotten a head start on eating and growing, so this little guy was a bit smaller. He was a little brother to both Omar and Olivia. What would be a good name for a little brother? It had to begin with an "O" because, after all, he was an osprey! With Omar as a big brother and Olivia as a big sister, Odie sounded like a good name for a little brother, so Odie it was.

Chapter 12

STANDING UP, WINGS, AND BALANCE

Bigger and bigger every day, they grew. Oscar and Olive were not the only ones who saw how big they were getting; Omar, Olivia, and Odie realized it themselves. When they would stand up and stretch up as far as they could, they could see out of the nest a little more each time. As their tiny bodies got a little taller and a little bigger, they discovered something else. They had wings! It was fun to stand up and move their tiny little wings at the same time. They were not only having fun learning about themselves, but they were starting to get exercise, which was very important. It would help them become strong enough to handle the big wings they would soon have.

Their feathers started coming in, and their wings were getting bigger than their small bodies. "Wow! How great are these!" they thought. "But how do they work?" They watched Oscar and Olive, and it wasn't long before they were flapping their wings, or at least trying! Every time each of them would give their big wings a try, they would fall forward, right on their heads. It was time to learn balance. Balance before flapping. Omar, Olivia, and Odie would soon find out there was more to life than just eating and sleeping. They had a lot to learn, and this was just the beginning.

Chapter 13

WHEN MOM SAYS HIDE, HIDE!

The bigger their babies grew, the more active they became and the more others could see them, too. Oscar and Olive had

to start teaching them how to protect themselves. Olive couldn't hide them anymore herself. They were too big. It was time to learn to hide. Hiding was very important at this very young age.

Whenever Olive felt like there was danger near, she would call out. Sometimes it was for Oscar to come, but it was also to warn her babies. Olive taught Omar, Olivia, and Odie to know that this call meant danger. It meant it was time to get low in the nest and to stay still. It was time to hide! Their new feathers were brown with white tips. This made it quite easy for them to blend in with the sticks and hide. When they would lie down and stay still, it was as if they weren't even there. Their colors made them look like part of the nest. It didn't take them long to learn how important this was. Now, when they heard the danger call, they would immediately get down and hide, and would not get back up until Olive gave the "all clear" chirps. If for some reason Olive had to leave the nest and Oscar was out fishing, she would give Omar, Olivia, and Odie the hide signal, and they would stay down until she came home and gave them the all clear sign. As long as they were hiding, Olive knew they were safe at home without her for just a short time. Hiding was how they would protect themselves from the time they were little until they could fly. Flying would be another way to protect themselves when they got older.

Chapter 14

THE JUMPING GAME

Soon, Omar and Olivia started to stand up, walk around the nest, and practice with their wings. Odie was not quite ready for all this. Standing up and trying to stay out of the way of all those big wings was enough. By the time Odie started doing more with his wings, they would sometimes hit each other with their wings. It was getting a little crowded.

Most of the time, it was Olive at home with them because, as usual, Oscar had to fish. The bigger Omar, Olivia, and Odie got, the more fish it took to keep everyone fed. At first, it was

only five or six fish a day, but as they grew, it took nine or ten fish to feed the family. When Oscar came home with a fish, Olive would still take it and tear it into small bites that her babies could handle and put the pieces directly into their mouths. Omar would always be up front. He was the first to beg and get the first bites. This explains how he was growing faster than the others. Then Olivia would eat, and Odie got what was left. This didn't bother Odie so much. He knew his mom would save him some. Odie was smaller and quieter than Omar and Olivia. Olive made sure they all shared and Odie always had enough.

Just one month after the eggs hatched, Oscar and Olive did not have babies anymore. They were young birds. Omar, Olivia, and Odie had gotten almost as big as Oscar and Olive. That's growing pretty fast! As far as flapping their wings, it didn't take long for them to be strong enough to do that. As a matter of fact, Omar found that jumping from one side of the nest to the other while he flapped his wings was a lot of fun. It was a big step. Olivia was always right behind her big brother when it came to trying new things, and besides, it looked like a lot of fun, so she tried it, too. They would each jump and flap their wings until they got tired, and then they would settle down to rest. When they were finished playing the jumping game, Odie would start playing, too. There was plenty of room for him then. To him, the jumping game was the best! Olive was always there watching each one of them learn different things in his or her own way. She was very proud of all three of them.

Omar, being the oldest, was always the one to try new things first. He left the jumping game to Olivia and Odie. He wanted to do more. He discovered that if he flapped his wings really hard

and then jumped, he would go straight up. He would go as high as one or two feet above the nest. This was almost like flying! Can you guess who tried it next? It wasn't Odie. It was Olivia. She watched her big brother all the time. She knew that if he could do it, she could, too. She didn't want him to get too far ahead of her, so she tried it. It took her a little longer to get it just right, but once she did, Olivia wanted to do it all the time.

Chapter 15

HOME ALONE

It had been about two months since Oscar and Olive had their babies. Omar, Olivia, and Odie were ready to get serious about flying. Watching Mom and Dad fly way up in the sky was exciting. Even Odie knew that if he was going to fly, he had some work to do. These days it wasn't very often that Oscar and Olive were both

home with the kids at the same time. There wasn't much room for flying practice with five full-grown ospreys on the nest.

Even though Omar, Olivia, and Odie were fully grown, Oscar and Olive still had to protect them.

They were still very young. Harriett Heron was always flying around somewhere and even had a hiding place on a board under the pier next door. Harriett Heron could no longer steal Omar, Olivia, or Odie from the nest for lunch because they were too big, but she would still make Oscar and Olive very nervous if she got too close. Oscar still spent most of his time fishing for the family, but he was always checking around for other ospreys that weren't welcome around Olive and the kids. But most of all, he was on the lookout for Harriett Heron.

Olive would now leave Omar, Olivia, and Odie in the nest alone without giving them the hide signal so they could have more room to practice using their big wings. Olive was never far away. She had two places she used to watch over her young birds. There was a flagpole right on the pier next to the nest. She spent a lot of time on top of that pole because it was so close. She would also sit high in the oak tree near the nest to watch over them. If she saw that danger was near, she would give the danger call, and Omar, Olivia, and Odie would all three immediately get down at the same time and hide. It was like all at once someone put a top on the nest and you couldn't see anything in it at all. It only took her seconds to fly down to the nest from the tree.

If Olive felt like there was real trouble, she would call for Oscar and he would take charge, chasing away the intruder. Harriett Heron was the most trouble. Even though Oscar chased her away many times, she would always come back to see how close she could get and what she could get away with, and she always made that awful croaking noise the whole time Oscar chased her. Fishing was important for Oscar to do, but he was always there when Olive needed him for other things.

While Olive was on the flagpole or up in the oak tree watching Omar, Olivia, and Odie, she could tell that Omar and Olivia were more serious about flying than Odie. Mom and Dad weren't home, and they had the whole nest to themselves. Odie was having a wonderful time jumping around. Once in a while, he would hit Omar or Olivia trying to use those big wings of his, but they didn't mind. They knew he was doing the best he could. Trying to do what Omar and Olivia were doing was playtime to him, but Omar and Olivia saw that their little brother was really learning to use his wings.

Chapter 16

FLYING

Flying, flying, flying! Other than eating, that's all they could think about. When Omar, Olivia, and Odie saw Oscar and Olive and the other ospreys flying around, they knew they wanted to

do it themselves more than anything else. Except for the white spots on their feathers, you couldn't tell the difference between Oscar and Olive and their three osprey children, except when it was feeding time. When they were hungry, everyone knew they were hungry! Getting bigger meant getting louder. Three full-grown ospreys all whistling and chirping as loud as they could to get some fish is pretty loud. And it didn't stop until everyone was fed and happy. They had become very noisy neighbors, but until they could fly and catch their own fish, chirping loudly was all they could do.

Omar had dreams of flying high in the sky, hunting for fish and diving down to catch the biggest fish in osprey history, and then eating it all by himself. Then he would go out and get another and another and another and always have all the fish he wanted without anybody's help.

Olivia thought of the day she would find a mate and fly around with him to help build a nest. She thought of having her own babies to love, protect, and feed just like her mom did for her. She would be the one that flew high up in the tree, watching her babies. She wanted to be able to fly down to them whenever they needed her. She wanted to show them how wonderful it was to be able to fly.

As for Odie—well, Odie was Odie. When he thought about flying, he didn't dream quite as big as Omar and Olivia. He just thought that if these wings were going to work and get him flying, he had his work cut out for him. He was as big as Omar and Olivia now, but he wasn't as strong yet. After all, he was the youngest. He would watch Omar and Olivia, and they set a very good example by practicing as much as they could.

The day finally came when Olivia and Odie saw Omar leave the nest. He was flapping his wings as hard as he could and he got almost five feet above the nest. He looked down at Olivia and Odie, then looked out across the water, took a deep breath, and said to himself, "Here I go." He went up and up and up. Omar held his big, strong wings out as wide as he could and found himself gliding through the air. It was wonderful. He had expected it to be wonderful, but this was more than he ever dreamed of. He looked down at Olivia and Odie, and they were still watching and whistling as if they were clapping and saying "Go Omar!" Their big brother was flying! *Wow!* Omar made one big circle, not going too far from the nest, and then another.

He decided this was enough for his first flight. He looked down and suddenly realized, "Oh no, now I have to land!" He decided to make another circle because he needed time to think. He had seen Oscar and Olive do it lots of times. How did they do it? He found a place that was bigger than the nest but close to it and decided it was a good place to land for the first time. It was the picnic table on the pier. If he missed the table, he would still land on the pier. He kept his eye on his new landing spot, made

sure his feet were down, flapped his wings really hard as if he was putting on the brakes, and he did it. "Look at me!" I don't know who was chirping louder—Olivia, Odie, Omar himself, or Mom, who had been watching the whole time from high up in the oak tree. Everyone was cheering. Omar was so happy and proud of himself.

Omar was standing there looking up in the sky, thinking about what he had just done and where he had just been, and he saw an osprey. This osprey was not only chirping right along with everyone else, but he was missing a feather in his left wing. It was Dad! Oscar had heard all the noise and came right away to see what was going on. Oscar saw that Omar was flying, and he stayed right there with him the whole time. Omar was so busy flying in the big sky that he didn't even see his dad, but he was glad to see him now. "Dad, I can fly"!

Chapter 17

DREAMS COME TRUE

This week was a very exciting week for this osprey family. Once Omar was able to fly, he didn't stay at the nest much. He tried landing every place he could and found it was very easy. You

wouldn't think that birds could put on the brakes in the sky, but they can, and they have to in order to land. Omar did enjoy sitting on the tree branch with his mom. He could look down on Olivia and Odie and see

what they were doing, and he could see his dad coming home with food. Omar looked forward to going hunting for food with his dad one day now that he could fly, but for now he would wait at the nest with Olivia and Odie for Dad to bring a fish. Mom was still in charge of feeding them.

Each day that went by, Olivia would watch Omar fly away whenever he wanted and sit with Mom high up in the tree. Each

day she would flap her wings a little harder and go a little higher right over the top of the nest. She wanted to fly away just like her brother did and know that wonderful feeling. She would look at the sky and say, that's where I want to be. One day Olivia flapped her wings as hard as she could. She started going up and up and up just like Omar did, and to her surprise, off she went!

It was amazing. Once she was up high enough and in the open sky, her wings just took over. All that flapping and jumping in the nest really did help build strong wings, and they felt great! She found that she could glide through the air without moving her wings at all, and when she did move her wings, she did it easily and gracefully. It was easy! Olivia was no longer just flapping her wings; she was in control. She was a beautiful, graceful bird flying high above water. This was a big part of her new life, the one she had dreamed of.

Chapter 18

CHICKEN

For the first time, Odie was alone in the nest. He wanted someone to come home. He looked up in the sky and saw Olivia

flying around and practicing her landings, and Omar was in the tree with Mom. Dad was out hunting for food. Everyone was doing something. Odie had to fly or he would always be left behind. Once in a while, he would feel sad and lonely

and would just sit there. He would think of how everyone left him, but when that thinking became daydreaming, he was flying way up in that big, blue, beautiful sky with the wind in his face.

It became harder and harder for him to just lie there. He wasn't going to be left behind! He had plenty of room to practice now, so he started practicing as hard as he could. He would have the strongest wings ever. He would fly, he would not be alone, and he would not be weak. He was a big, strong, beautiful bird, and he certainly wasn't scared. After all, he was an osprey, not a chicken!

Omar and Olivia wanted him to fly, too. They knew he wasn't a chicken, but he was the youngest, and it would take him a little longer to become as strong as they were. He just had to work at it like they did, and work at it is what he did. Now the only time he would just lie down in the nest was when he was tired from all his exercising. When it was feeding time, and Omar and Olivia would come back to the nest, Odie would jump up and start flapping his wings. He got so excited he would almost forget about eating. He wanted to show them how strong he was getting. Soon he would be out there with his brother and sister, his mom and dad, and he, too, would come back to the nest only when it was time to eat.

Feeding time was always the same. Oscar never stayed long. He would just drop off the fish for his family. It was too crowded for the whole family to eat together in the nest, so he would eat first, and then drop off fish for them. Olive would make sure everyone was fed, and then go back up in the tree. Omar and Olivia would stay for a while, but they would soon be off doing all the things ospreys do when they fly, and then Odie would be left alone again.

Odie had had enough. He decided one morning that this was the day he was going to fly. He was almost flying anyway.

With the nest just below him, he would flap his wings as hard as he could and get pretty high, about three or four feet, and then gently come down. Odie had watched Omar and Olivia do the same thing right before they flew off, so he knew he was ready.

He took a deep breath, closed his eyes—no, that was the wrong thing to do. He started again. He took a deep breath, started his engine—I mean his wings—and he started going up…a little higher…a little higher. Then he felt himself leaning to the right. The nest was no longer under him, and he started

to go down. The water was getting closer! *Oh no!* He flapped his wings like never before. Odie felt how strong they really were for the first time. He couldn't believe it. He started going up again, and within seconds he had control. Higher and higher, he felt the gentle breeze under his wings.

"These wings are wonderful!" he thought. Odie now understood why it looked so easy when Omar and Olivia did it—because it really was. His wings took over and everything felt just right! All his hard work had paid off. He wasn't daydreaming anymore; he was truly flying, gliding through the sky with the wind in his face, looking down at the beautiful water. He forgot about everything else and kept going and going until he realized he was still alone. He was flying like everyone else, but where were they? He was flying, and no one was there to see him. He wanted someone to see him! Then he thought of the wonderful story he had to tell, about how he almost went down in the water but at the last second caught himself and took off. It had been unbelievably frightening and exciting, and he had done it all by himself. He was not a chicken. He was a big, strong, beautiful, flying osprey.

Chapter 19

HOMECOMING

Flying for the first time was so wonderful! Odie didn't want to stop, but he decided it was time to go home before he got too tired. He knew that landing was next, so he had to save some of his energy for that. As he got closer to home, he heard whistling and chirping, and it was getting louder. He didn't give it much thought because he had to think about flying and how he was going to land. Soon the nest was in sight, and it looked like someone was there. As he got closer, he saw it was Omar and Olivia. They were looking up and whistling like two crazy birds. They saw Odie flying toward the nest. When Omar and Olivia had come back to the nest and Odie wasn't there, they became worried and hoped he was okay. They knew he had been left alone. Now Omar and Olivia were cheering. They saw that their little brother was fine. He was flying!

Odie saw them watching, and the thought of landing left his mind. He wanted to show Omar and Olivia what he could do, so he flew in a big circle high above their heads, chirping and whistling as loud as they were. "I did it, I did it!" That's all he could think as his brother and sister watched and cheered for him. When Odie came down closer to the nest, getting ready to land, Omar and Olivia both stepped aside to give him plenty of room. Odie glided in gracefully, put on the brakes, and landed as if he had done it all his life. The chirping got even louder. Omar, Olivia, and Odie were all together again and were very excited.

But where was Oscar? And where was Olive? As usual, Olive was not far. The nest was still home for these three young ospreys, and this is where they came for comfort, security, and

food. Olive still needed to be close by to watch over them. She had been sitting up in the tree and saw everything from the time Odie left the nest to the time he came back. Omar and Olivia had been chirping loudly for Mom because Odie was gone, and Mom was chirping to let them know she was there. That's what Odie heard when he was heading for the nest.

And what do you think Oscar was doing? You're right! He was fishing. He was flying off in the distance when Odie thought he was alone. Oscar saw that the nest was empty, he saw Olive up in the tree, and he watched Odie fly by. Everything was okay. Oscar wanted to be a part of the celebration, but he knew that when the excitement was over, they would all remember they were hungry. Olive came down to the nest because she saw Oscar returning with fish. Oscar landed with the fish, and just as he thought, they all remembered how hungry they were, so they turned to Mom. Olive fed each one, and as they got busy eating, it got quiet. Oscar stayed only long enough to be sure that everyone was okay, and then flew away.

He flew right above the nest to look down at his family and thought how proud he was of Omar, Olivia, and Odie, and how lucky he was to have the perfect mate. He thought back to the first sticks he had brought to the platform and how Olive would arrange each one to make their nest, and how they both fought for their nesting place and made it their home. He thought of how happy he and Olive were when she had three eggs and watched each one poke its tiny head out of its shell. When he couldn't be there with them because he was out fishing or chasing off intruders, he knew Olive was there. Olive fed their babies, helped to protect them, and kept them warm. As he looked down, he saw Olive and their children. He had such wonderful memories and a beautiful family.

Chapter 20

HUNTING

It was now time for Oscar to take over. One of the things that Oscar did very well was fish. Fishing was something his children had to learn in order to survive. It is natural for birds to hunt for their food, even if it is just an insect they are going to eat, but to fly above the water and dive for fish—that's pretty tricky. With powerful eyesight, strong wings, and feet with sharp talons, ospreys do it very well. It is just a matter of putting it all together and making it work. So Oscar first took Omar out to learn, because, after all, he was the oldest and the most experienced at flying.

Ospreys will often hunt in groups. They don't hunt near each other, but they do fly close enough so that if there happens to be a school of fish swimming by, they can share in the find. Omar soon found himself out flying not only with his dad but with other ospreys that knew how to hunt and catch fish. He watched very closely and saw how they would glide through the air and look down at the water as if they could see right through it, and when he tried it, guess what! He could see right through the water! Omar was just amazed at how powerful his eyes really were. He found himself just staring at the water, not sure what was going to happen next.

Then he saw a small school of fish swimming by. He started chirping, "There they are," and before he knew it, one of the other ospreys had dived down, grabbed a fish, and off he went. It happened so fast Omar couldn't believe it. "Wow! I have to do that!" About that time, he heard Oscar whistling. Omar looked over and he saw his dad dive down just as fast as the other osprey had, and then come flying back up with a fish. Omar was so excited to see his dad catch a fish! He looked down to see if he could see one for himself, but they were gone. As fast as they came, that's how fast the fish left. He realized he couldn't think about it too long—he just had to go for it. Oscar began whistling to let Omar know it was time to go home and feed everyone, so they both headed for the nest. Olive, Olivia, and Odie were all there chirping away when they saw Omar coming. They knew Dad

wouldn't be far behind with lunch, but they were also excited to hear about Omar's first time hunting.

Just as it took weeks to learn to fly, it took time to learn to fish. Olivia was joining her dad and Omar in the lessons, but Odie stayed behind. He wanted to go hunting soon also, but it wasn't time for him yet. They still joined together at home at mealtimes, chatting and chatting, whistling and chirping, excited about all they were learning and happy that Dad was still there catching fish for them.

Chapter 21

THE FIRST FISH

Odie was joining his big brother and sister when they went hunting now, but he stayed mostly with his sister. He thought his big brother would be too busy, so he played with Olivia. Learning was fun, especially when you made it a game. Together, Olivia and Odie would glide through the air and dive toward the water, pretending they were going to catch a fish. Seeing who could dive the fastest and who could get closest to the water was a game they played. Then, one day while they were playing, a big school of fish came by. One of the older ospreys dove down fast as lighting and grabbed one. It was the perfect catch. Then another osprey got one.

The fish weren't moving very fast, so Olivia started thinking she could catch one of those fish. She looked at Odie as if to say, "Watch this!" Olivia wasn't sure she would follow through with it, but she thought it would be good practice or a good trick to play on Odie. She dove down faster than she ever had before. The water was getting closer and closer very fast. "I can't stop now," she thought, and she could clearly see the fish. She had watched the other ospreys so many times she knew what to do, but could she really do it? With her eyes now on one fish, she decided to go for it! She stretched her feet forward, reaching out as far as she could to grab the fish. Then—*splash*—she hit the water. Even though she was in the water, she didn't lose sight of the fish. She grabbed it! Olivia had the fish!

She started flapping her wings to fly away, but they were in the water. It felt very strange. This had never happened before. She was scared and wasn't sure if her wings were strong enough to fight the water and get her back up in the air. Odie was watching from above and wanted to help his sister but didn't know what to do. He was scared, too! Olivia looked up and kept her eyes facing the sky, flapping her wings over and over as hard as she could and pushing the water with her feet. Finally she was free! She was out of the water. Olivia shook all over like a dog to get the water off and dry her wings. She flew higher and higher. She wanted to get away from that water! She flew right over to Odie, who was chirping with excitement. If he could have hugged his sister, he would have, but he needed his wings to fly. He was so happy to have her back with him and couldn't believe what he had just seen. Olivia had a fish! She did it!

In the struggle to get out of the water, she had not lost her fish. It was a pretty scary experience, but sometimes doing something for the first time can be scary. Now as she flew back to the familiar oak tree branch that her mother sat on so often, Olivia thought, "That wasn't so bad. As a matter of fact, it was great! I did it, and now look what I have!" She had her own fish to eat. She had been brave, and she was strong. She had taken everything she knew and learned and put it to the test. Just like her mom, she was going to sit on the branch of the oak tree and eat her fish, looking down at the nest that was her home. What a feeling! What a reward!

Chapter 22

ALL GROWN UP

Omar and Odie were home in the nest, chirping away. They were hungry and were waiting for Dad to bring them some fish. While they were looking for their dad, they saw Olivia up in the oak tree, eating. She had her own fish. This made Odie make even more noise. He was so proud of what his sister had done, and he wanted Omar to know. "I was there! I saw her catch her own fish!" Olive came rushing to the nest to see what all the excitement was

about and saw Olivia up in the tree. Oscar would be home soon with fish for everyone, but Olive went to sit with Olivia anyway. Just two months after hatching, Omar, Olivia, and Odie had learned how to balance, how to hide, and—each one in his or her own time—how to fly. These are all important things to learn and are a part of growing up. But now Olivia had learned to fish. She was learning to take care of herself, and that was a very big step.

Olive and Olivia looked down at the nest where Omar and Odie were chirping away. Just then, Oscar came with a fish, so Olive left Olivia and flew down for feeding time. While they were eating, Olivia flew off the branch and circled high above the nest. Looking down at the water, she didn't feel afraid anymore. Olivia had used her powerful eyes to see through the water. She had

used her mighty wings and felt how strong they really were. She was happy. She was so happy and sure of herself that she wanted to try one more thing. She made her way down to the water, and while she was gliding just inches above it, she let her feet glide though the water. This made her day complete. She had washed her feet, and this time the cool water felt so good! Her fear of the water was gone. She was in control, and she knew it. She flew off in the same direction she had seen her dad go, leaving everyone else at the nest.

While Omar and Odie were still busy eating, Olive saw all that Olivia had done and watched her fly off to join her dad. She had a very special feeling. It was a little happy and a little sad. Olivia could take care of herself now and was ready to start her life on her own as an adult osprey. She was all grown up!

Chapter 23

THAT FISH, ANY FISH

Omar had been hunting longer than Olivia, and he had tried catching his own fish, but hadn't yet. This didn't discourage him; he knew he could do it. Spotting the fish was easy, diving in the water was another thing, and then grabbing the fish and flying back up with it was a lot to do at one time, and you had to be quick. He knew it would take practice, but now that his sister had caught her first fish, he was determined to get his. "If she can do it, I can, too!" He was not going home today without a fish.

He was more determined than ever as he flew high in the sky, looking for a school of fish. Omar was so busy thinking about catching his first fish that he didn't notice that other ospreys were starting to fly in the same area as he was. He had found a good fishing spot, so now he just had to find the fish and catch it. Just then, he saw a large school of fish swimming by, and before he could get his thoughts together, another osprey dove down and got one. He made it look so easy. "I know I can do this!" Omar looked down through the water and followed one fish, thinking, "I will catch that fish." He thought of nothing else but *that fish*. He dove down to the water as fast as he could and stretched his feet forward to grab it. He didn't even worry about hitting the water; he had done that before. He just kept his eyes on *that fish* and, sure enough, grabbed it! As soon as he had it, he flew right up out of the water, chirping and whistling. Omar wanted the other ospreys to see he had caught a fish. He shook from head to toe to get the water off, and with his fish held tightly, he flew around whistling, "I caught a fish!" It was a very proud time for Omar.

When feeding time came around later that day, Odie was the only one at the nest. He was calling out for Dad. Olive heard

Odie. She knew what Odie wanted. He was hungry again, but she was more concerned with where Omar was. Oscar came back with a fish, and Olive and Odie ate, but still no Omar. Where could he be? Odie had had enough to eat, so Olive left the nest to look for Omar, and guess where he was? Omar and Olivia were out flying with the other hunters. Catching their own fish was going to be a big part of their day now. They learned that even the best osprey doesn't catch a fish every time. It can be windy, the water can be rough, and the fish can be too fast. Each time they caught a fish, they would learn another lesson. It would get easier and easier, and they would catch that fish or any fish!

Chapter 24

COME ON, ODIE

Omar and Olivia didn't come to the nest to eat anymore. They found their own special places to eat the fish they caught. Odie would go out hunting, but would always come home to eat, and Olive would still feed him, and then leave, and once again Odie would find himself alone. Being the youngest was sometimes tough because the older ones were always one step ahead. It seemed like he was always catching up. But on the other hand, watching others learn helped him to learn what was the right thing to do and what was the wrong thing to do, and if he ever needed help, he not only had Mom and Dad, he had a big brother and sister, too. Odie was thankful for all this, but he also knew what his next step was. He had to learn to fish.

He had gotten close to the water before—when he left the nest for the first time learning to fly and when he and Olivia would practice diving for fish. All he could think about was that he was a bird, and birds fly—they don't swim. The only way he would ever catch a fish was to not just get close to the water, but get in it. He had seen all the other ospreys do it, so he knew he could, too. Again, just like when he was learning to fly, he had to make up his mind that this was the day and just do it. Olivia had caught a fish on her first try, but Omar didn't, so whatever happened when he tried would be okay. The more he thought about it, the more excited he got. The water made the whole thing scary, but when he thought about the reward, he knew it would be worth it. He had been out flying with the other ospreys, watching them hunt and catch all the fish they wanted. Now it was his turn.

Odie had just finished his early morning feeding with Olive, and she left the nest. Odie watched as she left, and saw Omar flying by. Odie started chirping loudly, and when Omar heard him, he stopped at the nest. What was all the noise about? Odie was happy to see his brother. Although they were all flying now,

they didn't always see each other. Omar started chirping right back at his brother. It was just like when they were younger. "Isn't this fun?" Odie thought.

Well, it didn't last long. Omar had to say good-bye. He was hungry for his early morning fish, too. "Come on, Odie!" Odie knew just where he was going and really wanted to go hunting with his brother, so he followed him right away. He wanted to see his big brother catch a fish, and soon he did. Omar was getting very good at it. Odie watched everything he did. It looked so easy. It was a clear, calm, sunny, beautiful morning, and Odie made a decision. This was going to be the day. He wasn't hungry then, but he knew he would be later, and that is when he would catch his own fish. He spent the morning flying around, enjoying the beautiful day and getting more excited by the minute, thinking about his own fish!

Chapter 25

DAD NEEDS HELP

As the day went on, it not only got hotter, but it started getting windy. Odie went back to the nest, looking at the sky. Was there a storm coming? Should he go fishing like he planned or should he wait? He was getting hungrier. The weather was showing more signs of a storm coming. It was very hot and windy, and the clouds were moving in. He saw Olive fly by and land in the big oak tree. This gave him hope that Oscar would soon be there with a fish, and he wouldn't have to go fishing. He started chirping as he always did when he was hungry. Then he stopped. Was he going to let the weather be his reason for not going fishing when he had decided this would be the day? Again, he thought back to learning to fly. Was he an osprey or a chicken?

Just then, he saw his dad fly by. Oscar didn't stop. He didn't have a fish. He didn't even look at Odie or the nest. He was busy looking for fish. The wind had made the water rougher than usual, and that made it harder to find fish. Odie started chirping even louder, but this time he flew off to follow his dad. He was so hungry. He had to help his dad catch a fish right away. There was a storm coming!

Odie wasn't sure where his dad was going, but he knew he was a good hunter and would find some fish. Soon, he was flying over a shallow area of water that was protected. It wasn't like the rougher, deeper water. There were still some small waves from the wind, but in the shallow water it was easier to see if there were any fish. There were also more clouds now, but the sun would still shine through now and then. When it was shining, it was very hot, but it made it easier to look for fish with the sunlight on the water. Odie was so hungry, and the wind made him tired. He was just about ready to give up when the sun came out from behind a cloud and there they were, a small school of fish swimming close to the top of the water. Oh, they looked so good!

Odie forgot about everything else except how hungry he was and dove straight for them with his feet stretched out to grab the first fish he could. Before he knew it, he hit the water and had a fish. The fish were close to the top of the water, so he didn't have to go deep to get one. His wings hit the top of a small wave, but it was okay. The wave gave him a little push to fly back up. Hey, that wasn't so bad! As a matter of fact, that cool water felt really good. Next thing you know, Oscar flew down right where Odie had caught a fish and got one too. Flying side by side, they each shook the water off themselves, and Odie started whistling and chirping. Oscar did, too. Their fishing was done.

Odie stayed with his dad, wondering what to do next. He wanted to eat, but where? Did he have to go back to the nest? The wind was getting stronger, and it had started to rain. Oscar knew where to go. It was the place he would go when there was a storm, while Olive would stay on the nest to protect her babies.

They landed in the same tree, each one with his own fish. Odie had done it. He had gone out to help his dad, and that's just what he did. Oscar started to eat and looked over at Odie, who was eating as he had never eaten before. Odie had worked up quite an appetite, and his fish tasted so good! Was it because he was so hungry or was it because he had caught it himself? He didn't even notice the rain and thunder. Odie was there with his dad, and each had his own fish.

Chapter 26

THE NEST, THIS YEAR AND THE NEXT

It had been five months since Oscar and Olive started to repair and build up their nest for the season, and now their babies—Omar, Olivia, and Odie—were fully grown and taking care of themselves. They could fly and dive through the air. They could hunt and catch their own fish. They had learned about the good things and how to watch out for the bad. Now they didn't come back to the nest very often. Each one had found his own places he liked to spend the day and the night. Every now and then, one of them or Oscar or Olive would land on the nest because it was a nice place to land, but the nest was for laying eggs and raising a family. There were no babies anymore. The babies were now grown up and doing all the things adult ospreys do, including getting ready to fly south to Florida or South America for the first time.

Oscar left to go south first. Olive stayed behind just a little longer to watch and be sure Omar, Olivia, and Odie were okay on their own. She saw them flying gracefully as if they were gliding. She saw them fly fast like a streak of lightning when they would dive. And she saw them use their sharp, powerful eyes to hunt and catch fish even if the weather was a little rough. They were in control and each had grown up to be the big, strong, beautiful bird that the adult osprey is. Now it was time for Olive to go. She knew Omar, Olivia, and Odie would stay behind a little longer and leave when they felt strong enough to make the trip south.

She flew around one last time, whistling and chirping, saying good-bye and good luck to each of her children. She flew one last time over her nest with all the wonderful memories of her first season with Oscar. She had visions of meeting him there again next spring, repairing the nest after the winter storms, laying eggs, and again having all the joys of a mom watching her new babies learn and grow. Even though she knew she would never see Omar, Olivia, and Odie again, she had a good, happy feeling in her heart. She thought of how they would each find a mate and have a nest and babies of their own. She was a proud mom. As she flew off, leaving the Chesapeake Bay, she could hear ospreys chirping off in the distance behind her. Was it her babies saying good-bye? She wasn't sure, but she smiled to think it was.

It's well into September now, and the cooler fall air has arrived. Omar, Olivia, and Odie, along with the other ospreys, have gone. This is when the other birds start showing up. The seagulls start gathering on the pier where Oscar and Olive would sit to watch their babies. Harriett Heron loves being able to sit on the platform every morning to catch the sunrise, groom herself, and watch the world wake up around her. She spends most of her day flying around and finding new places to fish, and sometimes

in the evening she ends up here again. She will stay here a while longer. Edward and Edith Eagle now make it a stop just about everyday. They will start coming around now that the ospreys are gone, and will use the platform to eat, rest, or just enjoy the view of the little winter ducks that will be here soon and make a perfect meal.

When I put up the platform for the ospreys, I had hoped they would make it their home, and they did, but I have had a lot of other surprises. Other birds that live here have also used it, which makes it all the more enjoyable. So even though I felt sad when I realized Oscar and Olive and their three children had left, some of my sadness left when I saw the other birds come. This platform has been a success in a lot of ways. To Harriett Heron and Edward and Edith Eagle, it has been a place to enjoy while the ospreys are away. To the ospreys, it has been a place to build a nest, raise a family, and call home. And to me, the "Bird Woman,"—well, I can't express the enjoyment I have gotten. I have watched, I have learned, and I have grown to love those big, strong, beautiful birds. I feel like they are such a part of my life.

Even though there is still activity on the platform, when Oscar and Olive are gone, the nest seems very empty. The nest belongs to Oscar and Olive. The nest is where they will come home, year after year. The nest is where they will start a new season and lay new eggs. It will no longer be empty next spring, or the next, or the next. Oscar and Olive will come home, and it will once again be full of new life. And I can't wait!

Building an Osprey Platform of Your Own

Putting up a platform for the ospreys to nest on can be a wonderful project for you or your community. It can be something you design yourself, or you can follow the instructions found on the following web sites. Ospreys are not very particular. They just need a platform approximately 4 feet by 4 feet, and it must be able to support their nest. You also need to make sure the platform allows for drainage. Check out the following web sites for information on building two different styles of platforms. Get tips for your own design or follow their guidelines.

The Canadian Wildlife Federation, WILD Programs, "Habitat 2000/Learning about Wildlife: Lending Wings to Ospreys," 2000. http://www.wildeducation.org/programs/hab_2000/ activity/ospreys.asp.

The International Osprey Foundation, Inc, "How to Build a Platform," http://www.ospreys.com/ platform.pdf.

Fun Facts

> ➤ Regions where ospreys are particularly abundant include Scandinavia and the Chesapeake Bay.

> ➤ Ospreys have five different calls. These calls nearly always accompany a physical display. The different calls are used for begging, danger, courtship, defending the nest, and just because they are happy.

> ➤ Ospreys generally do not need to drink water. The fish they eat has enough water to meet their needs.

> ➤ Ospreys will eat their fish starting at the head and working down toward the tail.

> ➤ Young ospreys have orange-red eyes. Adult ospreys have yellow eyes.

➢ Young ospreys have white tips on their wings, giving them an almost spotted look. Their adult feathers replace their young feathers by the time they are eighteen months old.

➢ The osprey is the only raptor whose outer toes are reversible. The sharp, spike-like points on the underside of their toes allow them to hold on tightly to their fish in an aerodynamic way: head first, with two toes in front and two toes in back.

➢ When migrating, ospreys usually fly during the day. However, when crossing over the water, they will fly during the dark hours.

➢ During migration, ospreys fly an average of 170 miles a day, but they have been known to fly as many as 260 miles a day.

Suggestions While Reading

While reading *Oscar and Olive Osprey: A Family Takes Flight*, use this guide to promote conversation with your children or students. By talking about the story of Oscar and Olive's family and engaging in the suggested activities, you can help children express their thoughts, ask questions, and get involved. You can discuss the book while reading the story together, or talk to your children or students about what stands out to them as they read it themselves. Here are some suggestions to get you started.

➢ What has your older sibling taught you? What do you feel would be an important thing to teach your younger siblings?

➢ If you are an only child, is there someone older that you look up to and feel you can learn from? What makes this person special? Is there something that you feel you could teach someone younger who doesn't have an older brother or sister?

➢ What kind of example do you show so that others can learn from you?

➢ Was there ever anything new you had to do that made you feel unsure of yourself, or a little scared, but you did it anyway? What was it and how did it turn out? What could you teach someone from your experience?

➢ What do you dream of doing someday? Have you thought of what your life will be like when you grow up?

➢ What wildlife lives in your backyard or neighborhood? What does their home look like? How did they prepare a place to have their babies?

➢ Is there a particular animal, big or small, that you might like to learn more about, like another type of bird, a fish, or even a reptile?

Activities, Research,and Getting Involved

Putting up a birdhouse, a birdbath, or a birdfeeder is very easy to do and simple to maintain. This new activity will give you hours of enjoyment, and soon you will want to know more about the different varieties of birds that come to visit, eat, bathe, and make your backyard their new home.

The Audubon Society has books in every bookstore that are full of wonderful pictures and information. *The National Audubon Society Field Guide to Birds* is a great place to learn how to identify your new backyard friends. If you visit their web site at www.audubon.org and click on "Audubon Adventures," you will see their award-winning programs for grades 3–8. These programs are not just for bird-lovers; they also give you information about other wildlife. You can also find tips on backyard bird feeding and much more.

For more specific information on ospreys and other birds of prey through the Audubon Society, visit www.audubonofflorida.org. This is a web site that will introduce you to the Center for Birds of Prey. This center is one of the leading rehabilitation centers for injured or orphaned birds of prey (also called raptors). It also has a "Kids Corner" that has a monthly activity and new word of the month.

The Carolina Raptor Center is also great for information and activities. Go to www.carolinaraptorcenter.org and visit the "Kids' Zone." This page has fun games for elementary school children, activities for preteens, and science projects for high school students. There is even a section titled "Raptor Journeys." You can choose "Osprey Journeys" and learn about tagging ospreys to see the travel paths they take and the places to which they migrate. You can even choose a bird you would like to learn more about and follow it on its journey!

Animal Diversity Web is a web site from the University of Michigan Museum of Zoology. It is based upon work done by the National Science Foundation. It is truly an encyclopedia full of up-to-date information on many species of wildlife, and will answer all the questions you might have about any particular animal. The web site address is http://animaldiversity.ummz. umich.edu/site/index.html.

New Words and Phrases

Here are some words and phrases that will help you understand more about Oscar, Olive, and other ospreys. Following each definition is a sentence that uses the keyword.

Bird of Prey: a bird that eats meat and will hunt another animal for food
> An animal that is helpless or is unable to resist attack will become food for **birds of prey**.

Brood (verb): to take care of or give full attention to
> The female osprey will **brood** her babies almost constantly for the first two weeks.

Brood (noun): the young in a family
> Oscar and Olive had a **brood** of three this season.

Fledge: when young birds have grown their flight feathers and are ready to leave the nest

Parents continue to feed the young two to eight weeks after they **fledge**.

Pandion Haliaetus: the scientific name for the species to which osprey belong; there are four subspecies of ospreys, which are separated by geographic region.

The species that breeds in North America and the Caribbean and winters in South America (like Oscar and Olive) is **Pandion Haliaetus** Carolinensis.

Raptor: a carnivorous bird (see **bird of prey**), such as a hawk, falcon, or vulture

Because it eats fish, the osprey is known as a raptor.

Species: individuals having common attributes and designated by a common name

The osprey **species** is Pandion Haliaetus.

Talons: the claws of an animal or bird

Ospreys have unusually long legs for birds of prey, white feet, and black **talons**.

About the Author

Janie Suss grew up on the Chesapeake Bay in Maryland and has always been very active in the outdoors. The Chesapeake Bay is home to a wide variety of birds, including ducks, geese, swans, seagulls, herons, eagles, and ospreys. Janie's yard and pier are a welcome stop for many of these birds and a permanent home for others. Observing and researching them has become a passion, and she hopes that sharing this compelling story will encourage others to learn more about birds and develop a better appreciation for the lives of these beautiful creatures, as well as other wildlife.

Janie is number six in a family of eleven children, and has two children of her own, Gus and Sadie. In her writing, she draws similarities between her own family life and that of Oscar and Olive, teaching that even though they are birds, they seem to experience a lot of the same things we do.

Janie still lives on the Chesapeake Bay with her husband, Kip, and they look forward each year to Oscar and Olive's return.